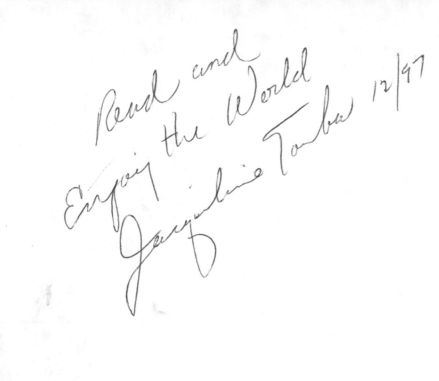

Read and
Enjoy the World

Jacqueline Touba 12/97

Young Artists of the World™
Ukraine

Sasha Kotyenko's Painting: "Embroidery Time"

Jacquiline Touba, Ph.D. and Barbara Glasser

in collaboration with the IACA World Awareness Children's Museum

The Rosen Publishing Group's

PowerKids Press™
New York

The young artist's drawing was submitted to the International Youth Art Exchange program of the IACA World Awareness Children's Museum.
You are invited to contribute your artwork to the museum.
For more details, write to the IACA World Awareness Children's Museum, 227 Glen Street, Glens Falls, NY 12801.
Acknowledgments: Maria Shust; Myron Surmach; Lubow Wolynetz; Yaroslava.

Published in 1997 by The Rosen Publishing Group, Inc.
29 East 21st Street, New York, NY 10010

First Edition

Book Design: Erin McKenna

Photo Credits: p. 4 © L. S. Williams/H. Armstrong Roberts, Inc.; pp. 7, 8, 16 courtesy of Tamara Kuzyk; pp. 15, 19 © Michael Reagan/FPG
International Corp.; p. 20 © Joe Outland/FPG International Corp.

Touba, Jacquiline.
    Ukraine: Sasha Kotyenko's painting "Embroidery Time"/ by Jacquiline Touba and Barbara Glasser.
        p.   cm. — (Young artists of the world)
    Includes index.
    Summary: The young Ukrainian artist, Sasha Kotyenko, discusses her culture and traditions, and describes a painting she made
    of herself and her sisters embroidering.
    ISBN 0-8239-5105-7
    1. Kotyenko, Sasha—Juvenile literature. 2. Child artists—Ukraine—Biography—Juvenile literature. 3. Ukrainians—Ethnic identity—Juvenile literature.
    4. Embroidery in art—Juvenile literature. [1. Kotyenko, Sasha. 2. Children's art. 3. Ukraine—Social life and customs. 4. Embroidery.]
     I. Kotyenko, Sasha. II. Glasser, Barbara. III. Title. IV. Series.
    N352.2. U38T68 1997
    947.708'6—dc21
                                                                                                96–54496
                                                                                                 CIP
                                                                                                  AC

Manufactured in the United States of America

Contents

1   My City   5

2   My Country   6

3   My Home   9

4   My Painting   10

5   Making Cloth   13

6   Embroidering Our Clothes   14

7   Women's Clothing   17

8   Our House   18

9   Traditions   21

10   A Country to Be Proud Of   22

Glossary   23

Index   24

My City

Vytayemo (veh-TAH-yah-moh)! That means "welcome" in the Ukrainian language. Welcome to our house in **Ukraine** (YOO-krayn).

My name is Sasha Kotyenko. I live in the city of **Kharkiv** (har-KIV). More than 1.5 million people live in this city. Kharkiv has one of the world's largest factories for making space rockets. Kharkiv is 70 miles away from **Kyyiv** (KEE-iv). In English, Kyyiv is called Kiev.

Kyyiv lies between the Baltic Sea and the Black Sea. It is the capital and largest city of my country, Ukraine.

Sasha
Kotyenko

◀ Millions of people live and work in Kyyiv, the capital of my country.

5

My Country

Ukraine is on the eastern edge of Europe. It is surrounded by seven other countries as well as the Black Sea. My country is about the size of the state of Texas. Over 50 million people live in Ukraine. Most of the people live in cities and towns. The rest live in **rural** (RUR-ul) villages.

In 1991, Ukraine became an independent country and Leonid Kravchuk became Ukraine's first president. For 70 years before that, Ukraine was part of a large country that was called the Soviet Union.

The Carpathian Mountains are in the western part of Ukraine. ▶

My Home

I live with my parents and my three sisters: Halyna, Tatyana, and Darya. We have a small house with a garden next to it. We grow vegetables, such as corn and beets, in our garden. My family likes to grow much of the food we eat. Outside the city, almost everyone has a garden.

Ukraine has some of the most **fertile** (FER-tul) soil in the world. The main crops that the farmers in Ukraine grow are sugar beets, wheat, barley, corn, and rye.

◀ Ukrainian families often work together in their gardens.

The window in my painting looks out onto our family's garden.

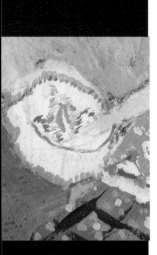

Can you see the tiny stitches and detail in our embroidery?

My Painting

I was twelve years old when I painted my picture. In Kharkiv, we have long, cold, snowy winters. During this time, my sisters and I stay inside and work on our sewing skills. In my painting, my sisters Darya, Tatyana, and I are **embroidering** (em-BROY-der-ing). Embroidery is a design or decoration that is sewn onto cloth with different colors of thread.

In my country, embroidery is very important. The neatness of our stitches, our choice of colors, and the patterns we make, tell what kind of people we are. In the spring, the young women of the village wear their embroidered clothing for everyone to see.

In my painting, you can see my sisters and me working on our embroidery. ▶

Making Cloth

My sister Halyna is spinning the fiber from a plant called flax on a spinning wheel. She is making thread. We use the thread to make linen cloth. You can see the thread piling up under Tatyana's bench.

We grow flax in our garden. After picking the flax, we soak it to get rid of the outside layer. The wind carries away the outer layer, leaving the inside of the stalk, called pith. Pith is the soft, spongy part of a plant stem. Thread is made from the pith.

To make these strong threads thinner, children swing on them. We weave this thread into linen cloth. Then the cloth is bleached white by the sun.

The thread that Halyna is making is under Tatyana's bench.

◀ My sister uses the spinning wheel to prepare the flax.

Embroidering Our Clothes

We embroider all of the clothing we wear for holidays and festivals in the evening after our chores are done.

We also embroider special towels which we put into our hope chests. A hope chest is called a *skrynya* (SKREEN-yah). A hope chest holds things that will be used for a young woman's married life. Some special embroidered towels are used in our Easter celebration. Others are for celebrating the birth of a baby and for weddings.

Ukrainians really like flowers. We grow them in our gardens, and we embroider flowers on our clothes, towels, and curtains.

Ukrainians have many embroidered things in their homes, ▶ such as the bedspread in this man's house.

Women's Clothing

Traditional Ukrainian costumes include many pieces of clothing. All of them are woven and embroidered.

First, we wear a long, white shirt called a **sorotchka** (so-ROCH-kah) with embroidery on the sleeves, the front, and the bottom. Our *sorotchkas* are so long they show beneath our skirts. We also wear a wraparound skirt called a **plakhta** (PLAK-tah).

We wear embroidered aprons over our skirts. The apron is called a **zapaska** (zah-PAS-kah). A sash called a **poyas** (POY-ahz) and an embroidered vest called a **kersetka** (ker-SET-kah) are also part of our traditional dress.

◀ The woman on the right is wearing her *sorotchka.*

My sister has the same type of embroidery on the sleeve of her *sorotchka* as the women in the photograph.

17

Our House

My father and his friends built our house. Attached to the front of our house are two posts that were carved by my father. He also made the *skrynya*, or hope chest, and all of the furniture in our house.

If you look closely, you can see that my sisters are wearing boots, called **choboty** (cho-BOH-tee). We wear boots inside our house because the floors in the village houses are made of earth. The floors become hardened as we walk on them.

Many Ukrainian families build their own homes. They are homes to be proud of. ▶

Traditions

In Ukraine, the men build the houses and make the furniture for their families. The women decorate the houses. My sister and I help my mother paint designs around the windows, on the walls, furniture, and *skrynya*. The *skrynya* holds our good clothing and fine embroidery.

We paint bowls and spoons, and at Easter, we like to decorate eggs with colorful designs. These eggs are called **pysanky** (PEH-sahn-kay). The inside of the egg is gently blown out through a tiny hole in the bottom. Every picture on the egg has meaning. My sisters and I learned how to dye and decorate *pysanky* from our mother.

◄ *Pysanky* are carefully decorated with different colors and patterns.

Our *skrynya* is covered with beautiful designs.

21

A Country to Be Proud Of

Throughout history, other countries have brought their traditions and ideas to Ukraine. But despite all of these outside **influences** (IN-floo-en-sez), we have always kept our own language, which is called Ukrainian. Ukrainian uses a different alphabet than the one used in English. The Ukrainian alphabet is called **Cyrillic** (sih-RIH-lik). The letters in a Cyrillic alphabet look different from American letters. We have also kept our **customs** (KUS-tumz) and beliefs. We are proud of our music, dances, and art.

I am always happy when I put on my embroidered clothing and dance in the village square during our festivals and holidays. I am proud of my country.

Glossary

choboty (cho-BOH-tee) Boots.

custom (KUS-tum) The way people have done things in a certain place for a very long time.

Cyrillic (sih-RIH-lik) How the Ukrainian alphabet is written.

embroidery (em-BROY-der-ee) Fancy needlework.

fertile (FER-tul) Able to grow things.

influence (IN-floo-entz) Having power over others.

kersetka (ker-SET-kah) An embroidered vest.

Kharkiv (har-KIV) A city in eastern Ukraine.

Kyyiv (KEE-iv) The capital of Ukraine.

plakhta (PLAK-tah) A wraparound skirt.

poyas (POY-ahz) A decorative band of fabric that wraps around your waist.

pysanky (PEH-sahn-kay) Easter eggs that are painted after the inside of the egg has been blown out through a tiny hole.

rural (RUR-ul) In the country rather than in the city.

skrynya (SKREEN-yah) A hope chest where special clothes and embroidery are kept.

sorotchka (so-ROCH-kah) A long shirt.

Ukraine (YOO-krayn) A country in eastern Europe.

Vytayemo (veh-TAH-yah-moh) "Welcome" in Ukranian.

zapaska (zah-PAS-kah) An apron.

23

Index

A
alphabet,
  Cyrillic, 22
  English, 22

C
choboty, 18
crops, 9
customs, 22

E
embroidery, 10, 14, 17, 22

F
flax, 13

I
influences, 22

K
kersetka, 17
Kharkiv, 5 10
Kyyiv, 5

L
language, 22

P
pith, 13
plakhta, 17
poyas, 17
pysanky, 21

S
skrynya, 14, 18, 21
soil, fertile, 9
sorotchka, 17

V
villages, rural, 6
Vytayemo, 5

Z
zapaska, 17